# When You Lose What You Can't Live Without

# WHEN YOU LOSE WHAT YOU CAN'T LIVE WITHOUT

*Identity Death and Renewal in the Wake of Calamity*

STEPHEN RICH MERRIMAN

 *Four Rivers Press*

SAN FRANCISCO, CALIFORNIA

BOSTON, MASSACHUSETTS

*www.fourriverspress.com*

Copyright © 2009 Stephen Rich Merriman

All rights reserved. Permission is granted to copy, quote or reprint portions of this book for purposes of review; for all other uses, contact the publisher through *www.fourriverspress.com*.

Book design by Tim Kinnel, www.wordsareimages.com

Cover art by H. D. Merriman. Used by permission of the artist.

ISBN 978-0-9817698-0-6

Library of Congress Control Number: 2008904322

**Library of Congress subject headings:**
1. Loss (Psychology) 2. Grief. 3. Bereavement — Psychological aspects. 4. Death — Psychological aspects. 5. Mental healing. 6. Self-actualization (Psychology).

*When You Lose What You Can't Live Without* ... is dedicated to all those who are, knowingly or unknowingly, engaged in the work of transforming fate into destiny.

# Contents

Foreword . . . . . . . . . . . . . . . . . . . . . . . .i

Prologue . . . . . . . . . . . . . . . . . . . . . . . v

The Nature of Identity . . . . . . . . . . . . . . . . . 1

The Convergence of Calamity . . . . . . . . . . . . . 5

The Scourge of Identity Death . . . . . . . . . . . . . .13

The Way of Quietude/Solitude . . . . . . . . . . . . . .19

The Current of Renewal . . . . . . . . . . . . . . . . .27

Paean to the New You . . . . . . . . . . . . . . . . . .33

## Acknowledgements

The author wishes to express his gratitude to the following for their steadfast encouragement and support for this book, sustained over a period of years. It is a blessed fruition of restoration, indeed, to have such wonderful family, friends and colleagues to draw on:

Emily Sara Taylor Merriman, Anne Allison, John Hallowell, Sidney Handel, Gloria B. Horvitz, D. Stewart Jester, Susan P. Lewis, Jeanne Lightfoot, Bill Ryan, Hannah Bigelow Merriman, H. D. Merriman, Joely Wilder Merriman, Edward Merriman, D. Cole Simonson, Johnn O'Sullivan, Stephen C. Simmer, Patrick Doherty, Charles Quinlan, David Seward, Vivian Walworth.

Special thanks also to H. D. Merriman for graciously contributing his original artwork for the cover of *When You Lose...*, and to Tim Kinnel for his creative and sensitive work in designing the layout of *When You Lose...*, as well as coordinating the production of the book.

Without the collective love and support of all the aforementioned, this book would not have been possible.

## Foreword

Everybody loses — no exceptions. To suffer a loss involving that which, to us, is indistinguishable from who we are is to suffer an egregious wound to soul and psyche—life-threatening to be sure. Indeed, *any* threat to personal identity is perceived as a threat of death, as a dynamic of dying. It makes no difference whether calamitous loss occurs through natural disaster or unnatural catastrophe, or involves the removal, from our lives, of another person through bodily death or emotional estrangement, or the loss of community, or career, or physical or mental capacities due to accident, illness, or advancing age, or the loss of material possessions, employment or financial standing brought on by economic hard times, or even the loss of cherished ideals — articles of faith once felt to be grounded in granite. Loss is loss.

Calamity and its attendant losses can be sudden or sequential, by leaps or increments, personal or collective, anticipated or through ambush. *No one is exempt from suffering them.* There is no immunity.

Perhaps more subtle are the attachments we make to those structural elements of our lives — those people, pursuits, stations-in-life, domiciles — which undergird and truss up the sheet-rock of our edifice of self. These are the "givens" of our lives — the "who we are" — and we rarely question our presumption of their constancy. Whatever, or whoever, these perceived givens of our existence may be, these are what, and whom, we assume, as a direct function of their constancy and our reliance on them, we can't (and will never have to) live without. They are psychologically and metaphorically our air, food and sunshine, our clothing and shelter; they comprise our very pulse.

Yet within the crisis of loss and the trauma of ensuing identity death brought on by calamitous events there awaits, for those who can withstand the process of material and psychological dismemberment long enough, an encounter with the ground of being itself—experienced as *both* the architect of calamity, and the soul-saver—the wringer of rearrangement, redemption, rebirth and restoration out of grinding and excruciating events. This encounter with the ground of being—the Self—is not—indeed *cannot*—be arrived at cheaply. The encounter awaits us, yet we know not where or when. Neither do we know the ultimate meaning behind such encounters, nor, at the outset, whether the ground of being be friend or foe—or both at once.

Any such concurrence—the encounter itself—is an experiential event that often defies pure logic and reason. It is a naturalistic phenomenon grounded in instinct and embracing the immediacy, "language" and trappings of instinct.

What this encounter with the ground of being, amidst the dying of one's former sense of self, seems to yield is a conscious rendezvous with a dynamic of rearrangement that is so fundamental and basic to soul and spirit life as to constitute some form of psycho-spiritual law, a law not rooted in abstruse concept, but planted stolidly in the viscera of instinctual ferment. This law, this intrinsic tendency, this principle of our being, *is* what both destroys us *and* redeems us.

It upends us and rips us away from "what we can't live without," and "we" die to our former lives. It strips and strains us, rendering to us, as a residue, our own indestructible essence, and then, after a purgatorial time "in the wilderness" (or the underworld, or the chrysalis), it, against a backdrop of what may feel like frightfully long odds, ordains the loosing of our essence on out into the world once again to attract to it that which is to become our new outer-world arrangement—the apparent resumption of our lives. Only from going through a rending-of-self, sufficient to lead us into a state of irreducibility in which we encounter, on the one hand, our utter impoverishment and, on the other, our meager, yet indestructible, sand-blasted, desiccated, rust-freed condition—only through such an ordeal can pregnancy, new moistness and flow arise, leading to a new emergence.

While such a process is not easily endured, if we strive to stay conscious of it, and of our place within it, at any given moment, great riches may await us. Cognitive, intellectual and emotional, material and spiritual life can finally catch up with, and even off, one another. We can come back into the world with a rich lode of reclaimed underworld veins and ores. To have died, gone into the wilderness, the underworld, and returned—not so much to tell the tale (for it is a tale beyond words, a tale before which words pale) as to incorporate it and exude it through our mere presence—is a redemptive passage for ourselves, and a kind of gift to the humanity which is us all. This gift is self-validating, highly visible to those who have already been obliged to undergo the torments, quite discernible to others who may be starting, under duress, in extremis and with protest, to open themselves to this process (or would, God forbid, aspire to it!), and helpful, overall, to the uninitiated, regardless of their level of awareness.

## Prologue

I write this to affirm what I have come through, and to establish my credibility with you, my dear reader and fellow traveler. When I was in my mid-forties, I was riding a crest which I had some reason to believe would carry me forward into my advancing gray-haired years. In retrospect, I suppose that I had achieved some measure of "conventional success." Though decidedly a late-bloomer, I had had a successful career for quite a long time, had hard-won expertise in my field for which I was receiving some recognition. Financially things had been on track for several years. My marriage, over two decades long, had much affection and a lot of seasoned teamwork behind it. Our older children were approaching college age, bringing new financial responsibility to cope with and lots of anxiety about all the big-time pressures that were upon me.

Yet we were a family, and I did have a career, and a marriage, and there was love in our house, and shared dreams ... and then it all crumbled away. I found myself subjected to attempts to discredit me within my career, which put my livelihood and my standing in jeopardy. This was followed by a protracted legal nightmare which, as I needed to defend myself vigorously against slanderous attack, defamation and character assassination, took time, energy and emotional resources away from my ability to be present to other, very cherished parts of my life. With my career in disarray and my life governed by maddeningly underhanded incursions and capricious rounds of legal jousting, a gloom descended upon me which would not be punctuated by any ray of sunshine. And then, well along in the process of career and financial dismemberment, and still gingerly feeling my way along treacherous legal shoals, my marriage dissolved. I both witnessed and experienced, at very close range, a progressive withdrawal of affection — the protracted, agonizing, incremental living death of well-honed intimacy and familiarity — the descent into alienation and estrangement, and the loss of the daily rhythms of family life. Emotionally ravaged, and frantic to stem the deepening financial hemorrhage, using a daring amount of borrowed money thrown into some "sure thing" served up by a new, ingratiating acquaintance, I found myself defrauded of this sum, with the self-serving friend having fled the state.

During this period I also endured a brief scare involving possible testicular cancer. Curiously, during the relatively short interval when the possibility of having cancer had not been resolved, I found myself very "ready to die." However, this readiness to pass on was anything *but* an outworking of spiritual maturity. Rather, as I sized it up, death by cancer would give me a "cheap out," with (apparent) dignity. While I was not frightened at the prospect of going, what *is* frightening, in retrospect, is that while still in my middle years (with so much of the potential of embodied life yet unlived), I had been psychologically and emotionally beaten down to such an extent that I was *so* ready to go.

Through being subjected to all of this, I learned the distinction that exists between being traumatized and being oppressed. To be traumatized is to suffer an acute, overwhelming indignity, often involving being hit blind-side. To be oppressed is to be *held down*, suffering a *series* of traumatic indignities, some foreseeable but others not, which have us at their mercy (without having our best interests at heart) and which will not let go until they are done with us—have had their way with us... and we are powerless to stop them. An oppression is a living, moving, ceaseless nightmare of repetitive inundation from which one can not awaken.

Collectively, these events, and a number of others besides (for example, the untimely death of my personally beloved jellicle cat Merlin, a steady soul-confidant and consoler while I was heading into the pit), occurring both simultaneously and sequentially over a span of five-plus years, constituted my calamity. Most everything that I had come to rely on as foundational and structural to life as I had come to know it, nurture it, cherish it and draw upon it prior to that time was dashed. I lost what I couldn't live without. "I" died.

While I know enough to realize that I am not uniquely afflicted to have suffered the extent of what was visited upon me during those dark years, frankly, I feel that I was visited by, and had to endure, my full share. Yes, I have broken bread with many who have, in terms of their external circumstances, suffered, in my estimation, far worse series of afflictions, both inner and outer, than anything I have had to face (and with them I would not trade places). And I read, daily, of the strife and tragic circumstances surrounding countless of humankind, caught in afflictions so severe I can't even begin to imagine withstanding them... On the other hand, no one among those who knew of the full extent of my unfolding plight felt motivated to come forward to volunteer to swap places with me, either (and I can hardly blame them).

Whatever my roster of afflictions, as best I can tell my own calamitous recipe was enough to open up—via means that were tailor-made for me—my own field of extended consciousness so that it could enter and taste, with some comprehension, the realm of human loss and suffering that forms one of the universal choruses punctuating human existence. I write this now having come substantially through the whole process of death → post-death (in the wilderness) → rebirth. There are, at this point (over five years into the process as I write this), clear lights discernible on the horizon for me, and I know now that I am on a glide path leading to a safe touching down in some new land.

Regardless of any theories I may have, I don't really know why I was obliged to encounter such protracted catastrophe, although as I have mentioned, I do know that I am hardly unique in encountering it. Whatever comes out of such a cascading demolition may still not be worth the pain that was exacted along the way, *but something has to come out of it, regardless.* Therefore, the whole reason I'm writing this book is to wrest something redeeming from the experience of having lost what I couldn't live without. *That* redemptive aspect will take on a more tangible reality for me if these words — and this brief, little book — can have a sustaining effect on the lives of other similarly afflicted people (of whom I know there are legion) who are in the process of actively undergoing the torments (or soon will be), as well as be of assistance to those who have already undergone the torments, and are actively delving them for meaning.

So may these pages to follow buoy you, oh you who are falling, or have fallen, into the slough of despond — whose life, as you have known it once, is ceasing, or has ceased, to exist. Our respective catalogues of worldly emotional, physical, material and spiritual dismemberments may not be exactly the same, but the contours of what it feels like, phenomenologically, to traverse psychological dismemberment and death, the shadow life, and the renewal into (a) new life are, as best I can tell, generally discernible and widely applicable, suggesting that the underlying process, regardless of individual differences and particularities, is, throughout, one and the same. As one common, unexceptional member of humankind who didn't, on the face of it, appear to stand a chance, and who has now, *mercifully*, made it safely across the great divide, I wish to set forth for you, after a fashion, perspectives on what it is like to undergo this process, and even speculate a bit, along the way, about what may be underlying it, and what it may ultimately yield.

Yours, with love and compassion,
Stephen Rich Merriman

April 26th, 2000
Shelburne Falls, Massachusetts

# THE NATURE OF IDENTITY
*Attachments Conscious and Unconscious*

Who are we, really? Whence ariseth the experience of "I-ness"—the tangible experience of who we are?

At every level of our being (save the very deepest levels which, wonder of wonders, are self-validating) we learn who we are through attachments—and attachments come in all sizes and shapes. There are attachments to people, attachments to places, attachments to things, attachments to situations, attachments to circumstances, attachments to institutions, attachments to environments, attachments to hearths and abodes, attachments to ideas or philosophies or beliefs, attachments to physical capacities, attachments to personal attributes in ourselves and in others, attachments to countless gods of our own conception, attachments to money, attachments to power, attachments to our standing within a community and to community itself, attachments to stations-in-life, attachments to life-roles, attachments to work and career, attachments to behaviors, attachments to indulgences of every description, attachments to family, attachments to friends, attachments to expectations as to how our lives will develop, who we "are" within our lives, and what our lives are all about (our personal myth). This list of categories of attachment could be greatly extended.

This is not to judge positively or negatively—or even neutrally—such attachments, or even the nature of attachment itself. We, each of us, are all amalgams of such attachments. Our personal identity, to the extent that we experience ourselves to be a *singular entity* (a polite fiction), is a composite of all the little components of identity contributed by each attachment. For most of us, only within the deepest meditation or while immersed in our deepest dream-life is it possible to have an experience of pure identity *as* pure being, and this experience is so participatory that the observing self collapses into it in a form of identity immersion. Yet this experience, though potentially instructive as well as highly validating, is *very* far removed from our day in, day out reality—read: our typical "experience of ourselves."

If our mundane, yet pervasively experienced identity is really a composite of our attachments, then, in a sense, we need all of these attachments to sustain ourselves as beings who are familiar to us. Any change in *any* of the attachments *is* a change in personal identity. In actuality, our identities are *always* changing, with "a little bit of this" attachment nudging out "a little bit of that" attachment, or a little bit of some new attachment rushing in to fill a momentary void stemming from a suspension or loss of some prior attachment, in a never ending sequence of identity alterations and evolutions. This process is typically so fluid, so incremental and seamless, that we are not normally aware of our own constantly changing self as "changing."

Perhaps thickening the plot a bit is the notion that although all of our attachments chip in their respective portion to our composite identity, we are largely unaware, within any given moment, of the *range* of attachments that exist within each one of us—which comprise each of us. Some major ones we can reasonably guess at, as in attachment to spouse or significant other, attachment to career, attachment to children, attachment to close friends, and so on. However, even in the attachments that we're capable of acknowledging, we typically have, within any present moment, a very incomplete notion as to the *depth* of such attachments, and hence only an extremely limited awareness as to the proportion of our identity—our being—which they supply us.

Compounding this quandary even further is the range of attachments we all have in areas of which we are *not at all aware*, the depth of which may equal or actually exceed the extent of our acknowledged attachments. These attachments of which we are normally unaware also chip in their portion to our composite identity, regardless of our lack of awareness about them.

Because of the range and depth of our attachments, both the known and the unknown-but-ever-operative, *we can never really make a reasonably accurate guess as to how loss will affect us.* We are usually too busy living within our assumed identity—being who we experience ourselves to be in the midst of what is also experienced as our unalterable matrix of attachments—to dare question the inherent instability of the ground on which we, in our experience of "I-ness," stand.

And then, life and fate—so intimately connected—do their thing, and we are plunged into calamity.

# THE CONVERGENCE OF CALAMITY
*Collapses Bidden and Unbidden*

Calamity is calamitous because of the forced removal of those attachments which comprise us. This removal of our identity-tethers leaves us stranded: twisting in the wind in existential angst, flimsily suspended over a yawning chasm, surrounded by fateful elements that do not appear to pay any heed to what we regard as our best interests.

Calamity is identity death—the loss of who we experience ourselves to be, both in the world and within ourselves. The loss of known attachments is heartrending enough, especially as such a loss awakens within us a realization of the extent or depth of such attachments, of which we were oft unaware. The more daunting and excruciating element of calamity, however, is *the rending of those attachments of which we have had little or no prior awareness as to kind and depth*, yet which have been profoundly operative within us, nonetheless.

What may start as a contained feeling of loss, powerful but not "self" threatening, may cascade into an exquisite rupture of torment—the upending and unwinding of "I-ness," as the heretofore unrecognized attachments are riven.

The actual question as to whether loss leads to, or becomes tantamount to, identity death has everything to do with whether such a loss involves the stripping way of sufficient attachments (whether of known or unknown lineage) that a kind of "critical mass" of identity formation is brought to a halt. From this point of view, calamitous loss is tantamount to those losses which reach, collectively, critical mass within the individual, leaving her/him stranded within the void of existential dismemberment—the "personal life myth" shattered. Losses stopping short of wholesale identity dismemberment are still wrenching experiences, but not calamitous.

Calamities arise in ways that may be at once seemingly random yet poignantly purposeful. Nor is calamity necessarily polite enough to confine itself, as an occurrence, to some well-designated demarcation within an otherwise tidy life, as in, for instance, that which is denoted by the well-honed expressions "mid-life crisis" or "mid-life transition." On the contrary, calamity can arise, without prior warning, anywhere and anytime along the span of life.

It is impossible to make even a representative list of attachments, the loss of which would be calamitous, because the range and scope of possible attachment are so extensive, on the one hand, and so individual—individual-izing—on the other. About the only guideline for briefly assessing the relationship between identity and attachment is this: *Wherever there is an imperative (and therefore an assumption) of unchangeability—of "being able to rely on," "being able to count on," "placing stock in," "having to possess or maintain"—together with a "knowing" that someone (or something) will "always be there (and in my corner!)"—an identity-contributing attachment churns just beneath the surface.*

It matters not whether an attachment carries an assumption regarding the constancy of an outer world circumstance (as in an established career or the presence of another person or other people in our lives), or whether attachment is "inward," as in, for instance, the assumption that our attractive features (whether of personality, appearance or physique) will continue to cast their spell and work their magic: attachment is attachment. Similarly, it matters not at all whether calamity involves the removal or loss of outer-world attachments (as in career, material possessions or people we love and have come to rely on) or inner/personal-world attachments (disruptions of our system of beliefs, or our personality, or the loss of our physical capacities or attractive features): calamity, in the sense that any such loss can lead to identity dismemberment, is calamity.

Calamitous loss is usually experienced as unbidden. In fact, it is often the apparent suddenness of an onset of loss, in the absence of our having any impending sense of its imminence, that can wipe us out at a single swipe. Then again, as previously mentioned, there are the anticipated losses which, much as we think we may have prepared ourselves for them, fake us out with their unexpected severity and our depth-charged reactions to them, and so decimate us. And then, moreover, there are those *sequences* of loss, starting with this assault compounded by that indignity and then this removal and then that blow, which take us apart piece by piece over extended periods of time — a true demolition of soul and psyche that eventually completely disembowels us.

These compounding losses engender a sense of dismay, a despairing descent into vertigo-of-soul. That which we thought we "couldn't live without" is stripped away or burned off in ways that seem utterly fateful. Either it's as if we are standing by the ocean shore watching, in transfixed disbelief, as everything we have been gets carried out to sea on a riptide (while being powerless to retrieve it), or conversely, it's as if everything we've ever been is safely upon the shore, and *we* are the ones in the riptide being dragged out to sea, watching with alarm as all that we cherish recedes in the course of our getting carried further and further out — and *knowing* that there's no getting back — no way to swim against the tide. We are cursed, and "in for the duration," and we know it.

And what can be said of "bidden" losses? On the one hand such a notion—that of conspiring to lose because we actually want to—seems idiotic. And from the ego—"I-ness"—standpoint, it is. Who would, in the midst of an apparently successful, relatively stable, productive life *knowingly* choose to court calamity—to court identity death!? (No one of my acquaintance.) Those of known suicidal bent may appear to contradict this point. However, it's important to bear in mind that those who are knowingly and willfully suicidal have *already*, within their mode of experiencing, encountered calamity of one form or another sufficient to rend them from their attachment to their lives as who they once were. Once upon a time, prior to their own rendezvous with calamity, they did not maintain the volition of suicide. (The real tragedy in such cases is that the urge to suicide, more often than not, goes unacknowledged in terms of its *psychological* significance, and the relevant challenge—the *inner* drama—of submitting to the process of psychological death and rebirth is, in the absence of this recognition, given literal, grotesque, concrete expression in the form of terminating bodily existence.)

If our ego-self is, amidst a flourishing life, an unlikely candidate at the feet of which to lay blame (to place responsibility for these machinations of our undoing and demise), are there any other elements of our being that could be capable of doing the bidding—of "bidding for calamity?"

Probably. Human consciousness is pluralistic, and those parts which comprise us (or, from *their* perspective, those aspects of *their* totality to which we, in our "I-ness," contribute) are decidedly autonomous, functioning outside the realm of our conscious intention and having, in fact, conscious intentions and designs of their own. Indeed, what is primarily *unconscious* about our "unconscious" is not necessarily any unconsciousness *within* it, but, rather, *our own unconsciousness of it*.

To the extent that we are open to receiving glimmerings of behind-the-scenes intentions, we may sometimes observe a larger picture — the picture that, though including us, is larger than we, in ego form, are. Such glimmerings, if we are receptive to them, can come to us through dreams, intuitions, meditation, the impulse to engage in artistic creation and expression (in any modality), and synchronicitous events reaching us from the outer world which reveal unlikely, yet definite, often uncanny connections between our inner and outer worlds, and thereby get our attention. The conscientious opening of our puny ego-hood to these channels of expanded awareness, perspective and design will oblige us to confront — not by way of being confrontational, but by way of encountering — many sides of "ourselves" (our "selves") which appear to be carrying on their own lives and missions regardless of our own sense of urgencies, priorities, virtue, and, yes, attachments.

One useful way to consider this is to, at least hypothetically, regard these many sides of ourself as *simultaneously* seeking some form of life — of living, corporeal existence — through this one physical body "we" all share. If we (the ego standpoint) have constructed rigidities in our lives which sufficiently truncate or frustrate the ability of these coexisting consciousnesses within us to find suitable manifestation or expression in material/corporeal existence, then no matter how well established our life-edifice in the material world may be — our attachments to people, time, money, standing, career, and so on — these coexistent consciousnesses *must* — can't help but — have a vested interest in upending us so that a new possibility, birthed out of the rubble of ego-identity death, can come into the foreground in which "they," in some combination, can find embodiment and expression—the better that they may realize greater corporeal life.

It can be truly unnerving to reconnoiter the actual autonomy and apparent cross-purposes to which "we," in our larger pluralistic sense, knowingly and unknowingly (unbeknownst to us in our more limited sense of "I-ness") work. In our more limited ego frame we reflexively hijack our body—perhaps our most powerful worldly attachment—and then, under the implicit presumption that we (in ego form) are the body's only occupant, ground our self within it by shooting out tendrils of attachment everywhere. Yet these additional, ignored or disregarded coexistent sides of us (or are we sides of *them*?), having been straight-jacketed out of our corporeal mix, bide their time and, ultimately, plot our undoing. They *must* do this for, not unlike us within our own, relative ego standpoint, they, too, have their own sides "to whom to be true." They regard us, in our own ego-form, as peripheral players in *their* own drama, and not necessarily as central characters or, sometimes, of even marginal importance (beyond our own de facto attempts to marginalize or disregard *them*). To the extent that "we" obstruct or impede "them," and their flow, we—and what they may regard (from their standpoint) as our constricting life structure, no matter how dear it may be to *us*—are expendable.

Our overall unconscious, *in its unacknowledged, disregarded and unhonored plight*, is simply that harsh in its view and assessment of us, as we carry on in our single-handed, headstrong fashion. Given this heavy-handed egoistic state of affairs, our unconscious, in the fullness of time, deals with us accordingly—and thoroughly.

# THE SCOURGE OF IDENTITY DEATH

*Dismemberments Broad and Deep*

The nature of identity death cannot be objectified because the death of identity is the death of that faculty holding the capacity to objectify. Within it, logic and our descriptive objectivity collapse. Notwithstanding the impossibility of rendering a discursive, process-oriented description of identity death that could carry with it any convincing depiction of the breadth and depth of the experience, it is possible to attempt to render a semi-phenomenological account of it. Such rendering is utterly unscientific and thoroughly subjective, utilizing — relying freely upon — metaphor and analogy and "it's-as-ifs" to seek to convey some resonance of the overall experience. The attempt to make a translation of such a phenomenon into language is also necessarily limited by this writer's capacity (such as it is) to be able to employ language, and the written word, in a manner that is sufficiently evocative as to render some sort of impression of it. Such a task is daunting. However, since verbal language is the medium (in this format) in which a translation must happen, what follows is this writer's honest attempt to harness it in service of conveying — of making a translation of — subjective impressions of one version of the identity-death experience.

Identity death is the loss of air, food or sunshine — that which used to nourish us. Identity death is finding ourselves no longer able to breath familiar air, to eat familiar food, or to find happiness in familiar things or places or people. *Our cherished ways of coping — no matter, historically, how well seasoned, well worn, reliable or proficient — are of utterly no use in dealing with our tragic collapse.* Our well-honed, trusted ways of dealing only have the effect of compounding our tangle of demise if we continue to utilize them.

Identity death is irreversible. It is the loss of that which so defined us. We are rebuffed, thrown back, exiled, panic-stricken, bereft, gasping, depotentiated, shut-off, cut off, cast out, thrown out, dragged down, dragged under, held under, bled dry, expired. We collapse into ourselves and find nothing, within, to fall back on—nothing within to cushion our descent—nothing within with which to upholster any definition of some future hope or possibility. There is a sense of alienation from ourselves and from all things. We are soul-nomads—soul ghosts.

Words come not anywhere close to rendering a fair impression of the exquisite, unrelenting soul-torture of identity death. We are torn away from all anchorages, stable moorings and safe havens, treading gingerly at the mercy of external, fateful ravages and inner, unceasing self-inflicted indictments and torments. Our hostile fate, as a final indignity, keeps us bodily alive, that we may be forced to bear the excruciating consciousness that Life, as we once knew it, has ceased to exist—that we, as we used to know life, have died.

There is the loss of former abode, of a sense of hearth, of emotional repose and safe-keeping. We are estranged or exiled from all that was once assumed and familiar. There is no refuge, no sanctuary. All heroic or noble illusions have collapsed. We are slain. Life force is expelled; deflation is everywhere. A nameless presence peers out through these weary eyes and witnesses the dissolution—everything so once known and cherished, and now so gone. Lots of familiar outlines hold nothing, any longer, within them. No resources; no reserves; no rescue. The breath is shallow and quick. The chest collapses under the weight of a thousand atmospheres. We are made to gargle molten lead. Death envelops us. With consciousness to know, yet with no power any longer to fend off, we collapse into it. And even as we collapse, there is no surcease: there is only this one, true emotion of finality. Beyond all tumult, we are riven. We are done.

The past, as a repository of former happiness, haunts us in our dismembered state. The exquisite torment of what once was, but no longer abides, is our constant companion now. As disemboweled, disembodied consciousness, we live in an ambulatory half-life Hell of crushed dreams, lost, diminishing or spent physical capacities, every breath an ache, every moment a new punctuation in a nightmare from which we can not awaken. Spikes are driven through us all over, but no blood flows; the blood has already left; no blood flows from a cold bled corpse. Gradually, our souls freeze, our energies, scattered, dissipated, are cast to the four corners. In the frozen hush, a desiccated husk is all that remains. The shriveled soul-stench of death, hanging over us as a final dissolution — one that is beyond any bargaining or redemptive potential — overtakes us.

No attempts to bargain budge death: the experience is unconditional. No apparent positive efforts, or appeals for clemency on the basis of past nobleness of intention, dissuade it. Bleakness is the one engulfing reality. And Death's most apparently convincing message is this: we are to stay suspended within it through all of eternity. It is "the final word" on us — one more tragic life notched up — one more spent carcass tossed upon the rotting heap of the tragic. And so we enter death and, living in the presence of our own death, a numbing stillness — a stilling numbness — overtakes, suffuses and dissolves us.

Somewhere within these clutching words, scrawled while revisiting the throes of the very state they attempt to render, wafts a vapor of what it feels like to be carried into the experience of ego-identity death, as precipitated by wrenching, cascading unanticipated rupture and loss.

# THE WAY OF QUIETUDE/SOLITUDE
*Wildernesses Within and Without*

Beyond all angst of loss and dying comes the emptiness—the opening to the expanse of inner and outer wilderness—soul limbo of suspension between two worlds: one, now stripped bare and receded, the other—shadowy—a future yet to take form. The carnage has stopped; the rest of the passage remains.

Betwixt these two worlds is a formless and aimless region, a state of being *initially* devoid of meaning—devoid of having its own qualities as distinct from being describable other than in negative terms—as being "a lack" of this, or "in the absence" of that. Solitude/quietude prevail. In this space and time beyond identity death, there is, discernibly at least, purer awareness despite what appears to be a lack of much substance. We still "are," we exist, we still "be"—but we are unadorned with outer trappings or internal referents, our accustomed points of self-orientation.

Wildernesses are first experienced in their strangeness. The sense of foreboding which accompanies this strangeness is not that something may happen or befall us—such would no longer be consequential since we're already beyond dead. The foreboding of strangeness is, rather, that *nothing* further may happen to alleviate, or at least lend direction to, our condition. All in the outer world—the more normal trappings of significant other(s), career, activities, social life, et al.—are either gone or apparently permanently receded. The more normal staples of our inner orientation with ourselves—the assumed and formerly unquestioned gestalt of who we experienced ourselves to be and *knew* we were—these formerly internalized identity tethers are no longer operative. We are whoever we are without, any longer, traditional roles to define us.

So what is "wilderness living" really like? For one thing, it is living more on essentials and less on excess—on conveniences. It is meeting basic needs in the hopes of making it through another interval—another morning (mourning), another afternoon, another night, another day. It is being in the present, in which there is *lots* of presence and seemingly very little defined being. It is to begin to know a region which is perceptible only through and beyond death—identity death—much as a frozen river in the dead of winter opens to adventurous skaters a marsh that would not, otherwise, be accessible at any other time or through any other means. It is to begin to recognize the strangeness and untamable wildness in all things familiar, and to find a basis of familiarity amongst all things wild and untamed. "Wilderness" living comes to place an emphasis on exploration for the sake of exploration, rather than on being in quest of any particular discovery. In wildernesses, both inner and outer, we "go native."

So here we are, suspended in a chrysalis between "we-used-to-know" and a future "I-can't-imagine-what." There is something in wilderness living that serves the rearrangement of that which comprises us. Like the initial steaming issuances of long-dormant calderas underlying snow-covered slopes, long-forgotten, atavistic, instinctual ways of knowing and perceiving slumber awake. One can hear a thickening layer of ice holding conversation with itself (or is it with me?) on a frozen, windswept pond. One can begin to smell a pavement while walking, to sense the groaning earth as it yields to the impetuous sprouts of a new spring. One can feel the rumblings of ten thousand diurnal rhythms pulsing ceaselessly through creation. One can find solace in leaning against a tree with the breeze in one's face. One can immerse oneself in a moment of pure being in befriending an unknown neighborhood kitty for whom the world still works as a tamable domain. One can observe, and witness, and *feel*, the striving and the risk existence holds for all creatures upon the earth.

Wilderness living is "doing-for-the-sake-of-doing," "being-for-the-sake-of-being," all the while learning—initially in the course of killing time—how to *ride* time. Wilderness living is the development of keen perception, and the awakening of an awareness that through the very act of perceiving, we are in relation to all that we perceive—*no* exceptions. In the absence of any felt sense of personal future or destiny, wilderness living begins to be an existence that is outside and beyond any personal future or destiny.

Wilderness living is not simply finding untrodden-upon nature to inhabit: it is a composting in which our *own* battlegrounds—both inner and outer—decompose into organic matter which starts to fertilize and refoliate them—transforming them into composted, bucolic settings of quietude, retreat, solitude and sanctuary. Within these settings nature—the *wildness* of wilderness—can once again claim us.

Wilderness comes to us; we don't need to seek it. The backscratching elegance of bark on an old tree, the creaks and pains of still-aliveness within our own bodies, the gentle undulation of a chorus of trees feeling and swaying before the ancient wind, the sudden surfacing of unexpected personages aimlessly crossing our path, charged at once with momentary, potential meaning even as they hold none—a fox, close by, so utterly unperturbed by an urban environment, nonchalantly trotting past, sauntering along on his nightly rounds; little green shoots finding and then extending a foothold (a root-hold) in massive, manicured, stubborn concrete (you know, in the end, which will win that standoff!); magnificent, ancient Orion rising full-bodied in the East to command a crisp, ink-black, winter canopy of sky—*wildness enters everywhere.* Old places haunt us, or do we haunt them? Are they our "old haunts," or are we "their ghosts?" Have *we* become the wildness in them?

The wilderness experience holds yet another fullness just waiting to be stumbled upon. All those concentric layers of previously unmanifested selves within us—within our pluralistic psyche—converge in the present moment. The pure present is the meeting point of all these possibilities as they exist *simultaneously.* This is why the present, in its essence—our essences—is so unstructured, and must necessarily be. To move to impose structure prematurely on the unbounded present is to move to favor one side of ourselves at the expense of all the others—to crystallize, or precipitate out of the boundless mix, one lopsided extract only. To engage in this would lead to yet another unbalanced manifestation of self in the outer world. Even if this new "self" were quite different from what preceded, it would likely be just as out-of-kilter. Therefore, moving to force the present moment into a premature yielding of structure—with its train of attachments and the resultant truncated identity that would follow—is less than optimal.

*To knowingly tolerate and start to befriend the present moment in all its latent but felt fecundity is the essence of wilderness living.* In the true present *everywhere* is a wilderness, and our many denizens of self are continually poking their heads out through the underbrush to greet us in one form or another. Our wilderness home is a "room with many mansions" and, as an inner abode, it creates the "home" sense—the sense of hearth, the sense of a place of utter familiarity and belonging—*regardless* of wherever in the outer world we are sheltered or choose to lay our head. All sense of "home" originates *here*.

The registering of layers of uncollated impressions in a mosaic of randomness and pattern — days upon days, maybe months upon months (even years upon years?) — all this and more — or is it less? — seemingly without beginning, without end — life-as-interim-only, and yet in the interim lying *all* — all in a suspension of the indeterminate sentence "a-day-to-life" — this is life in the wilderness.

What, if anything, can begin to take form from this suspension? ... within this wilderness? ... in the Underworld? ... within the chrysalis? For a long, long time, maybe nothing ... *And yet*, if the wilderness experience means anything at all — if it ever points to anything beyond itself — the time in the wilderness, *whatever* form it takes, has everything to do with a rearrangement which will, at some point, place us out into the world once again. Or perhaps it would be more accurate to say: "place the we that we are becoming, are meant to be — an arrangement of 'we' in which other sides of our collective 'self' can find expression within the body — on out into the world, once again."

It is only in the experience of being restored or refashioned and then again *launched* that prior identity death and consequent wilderness living can most fully reveal the magnificence of the process which underlies them and which has possessed us — the cosmic law to which we have been forced, in terror, to submit, and which now, in true revelation of the once hidden agenda behind this law, starts to buoy us up and direct us *outwards*. Within such a process, there is nothing necessarily magical about time — only *timing*. We begin, by fragile minutes and humble degrees, to anticipate — to *feel* the anticipation of — the emerging from the chrysalis, the ascending from the underworld, the finding of our way back into communal life from a wilderness which we have, in the interim, come to know and, after a fashion, befriend. We start to feel the readiness for our return, not as a deliverance from an exile or the commutation of a sentence, but as a journey-of-return from rarefied territory that we have, to an extent, explored, and from which we now carry forth great riches ... for we have lived to tell the tale. Our return is not a retreat from wilderness: it is an *enlargement* of it, a placing of us back into the world in a new, yet-to-be-revealed way, tweaked with our freshly minted ways of knowing and perceiving and experiencing—and incorporating—as a new "we."

# THE CURRENT OF RENEWAL
*Wildernesses Endured and Transcended*

At first, even the *thought* of rebuilding engenders instant exhaustion. The very notion of having to start over—of having to do *anything* other than just make it through another day—incurs a paralyzing entropy. Yet Renewal is ineffable. It reaches us despite what may be our own deep-seated convictions that it is not possible—that we just don't have it in us. The Universe, however, is simply not through with us (as remarkable, at times, as *that* may seem). Transition, Restoration, Anticipation, Hope, Freedom, Gestation, Patience, Innocence, all these qualities (and so many others, besides) are intimately entwined with Renewal, helping, within their entwinement, to make its contours discernible.

Within Transition, the perspective that we have been, and are, intimately involved in the archetypal passage of Death → Rebirth becomes, in hindsight, clearly recognizable. With Restoration comes the conviction that we are starting to receive "divine" inheritance—that we are in the process of becoming—*not* the person we should have been, or had to be, or wanted to be, or must be, but, rather, the person we were *meant* to be. This conviction arises amidst what may often appear to be the absence of any apparent affirmation in the outer world that restoration is occurring. Yet the incremental influx of Grace becomes, by degrees, too pronounced to be doubted. It is an immanent, *felt* reality. Anticipation arrives as a sense of expectancy, less any *specific* expectation. It's its own kind of climate—a background watercolor wash gently influencing the appearance and migration of other shapes, forms and colors into the foreground. Hope carries within it the aspiration that this rebirthing and restoration of ourselves that we sense is somehow in the works may lead to a flowering in the outer world. Hope steels our spine with renewed resiliency and determination. It says: "Stay tuned: stay in tune—attuned." Freedom becomes known as the flip side of loss and attrition. All that superfluous stuff, once experienced as so essential and indispensable—as indistinguishable from "I"—has been boiled off during our spell in Hell. Spiritually we are tougher, leaner, meaner, more sinewy, resilient and ornery—full of gristle. The essential, irreducible "I-that-is-we" has made it through the sawmill—*and* the sawdust pile—intact. We exist within an envelope of receded former-life obligations, responsibilities and identity, and yet-to-be-revealed-and-chosen identity, structure and form. This interim freedom of burdens-in-abeyance is remarkable to encounter and contemplate. Our identity, a "peeled zero," is womb-like. Within it, just beneath the surface, we are pulsed by our pluralness of being, so much of which, now competing for manifestation, is seeking to be shaped and assembled into birthable form—included in the mix of what is to find realization and expression in our soon-to-reassemble life structure. Gestation, the simultaneous ripening of, and awaiting, new life, is all about us—all in, through, and around us. We "ride time," knowing that a fullness is in preparation for birthing, and sensing that *this* fullness is not simply something that is happening to us, but is, rather, who *we* are becoming. Patience, that old-fashioned virtue, is no longer a clenched-teeth experience. We know the trick of harnessing time in service of furthering our to-be-revealed identity and destiny. *There is no sense of hurry.*

Everything that is to come to us is to come to us anew—either *as* new, or as some former something arising in a new way—minus *any* struggle to short-cut our way into some novel refrain of "same old" constriction-based security, and less any effort to clasp that which was earlier removed from us. And Innocence, that unfettered, agenda-free way of experiencing the effulgent fullness of the present moment, embodying a child's wide-eyed curiosity and fascination with any immediate discovery of the new, in which the unexpected lurks and crouches in potential kid-ish ambush around every corner and behind every shrub, suffuses our being, revealing Reality as consisting of quirky, squishy, coquettish, non-linear stuff, bursting with possibility, and demanding of us astonished, open-ended receptivity to whatever is developing within us, and whatever we are encountering "without" us. All these qualities (and many more, besides) form part of this slurry called Renewal.

Renewal is tidal. We are carried along on it. We feel its swell starting to lift us, and we catch a wave. We may learn to navigate our course upon it and to shape it to some extent, but we do not create it. It puts *us* in motion: it re-creates *us*.

Paradoxically, one of the distillates of Wilderness Living is the recognition that a range of attachments has actually survived identity death. These attachments, which prior to calamity may not have been particularly recognized or valued (occluded as they were by our then more strongly prevailing attachments) have *not* been lost in the scouring of calamity. What a discovery! The surfacing of a survivor-set of attachments is not simply a case of "Be thankful for small blessings" (even though we may be), or the conjuring up of some other maudlin sentiment. This surfacing is the beginning of the reacquisition and reprioritizing, as a first movement, of that which has been previously ignored or neglected, and which now may come-to-matter. This development—having its roots initially within the wildness of wilderness living—is the first nudge of a retrieval of, or opening to, something of our past that can actually be brought forward. The operative prayer which frames such a revivifying current goes something like this: "Thank God for what I've got ... for what I've left behind ... for what is coming back to me—and forward with me."

Renewal, far from being announced by a starter pistol's report signaling the end of Wilderness Living and the beginning of something else (although even *this* is possible), often commences as a barely discernible outgrowth of wilderness—as a gradual triumphing over our own estrangement and sense of self-banishment, alienation and exile, of being at the mercy of the inimical and the unfamiliar. Our feelings of singular loneliness and isolation and of being "at risk" start to give way, bit by bit—to evolve into a befriending of a simpler, more open and openended "we." Loneliness becomes tempered with not-aloneness, and our sense of isolation is gradually supplanted by a recognition of our elective solitude, on the one hand, and, on the other, elective (if initially very brief) engagement, in some fashion, with the outer world. Our sense of being at risk mellows more into a benign coexistence with that which lives in the dark. Night and darkness are no longer our bane. We lose the torment of fright, and we gain a new, more gracious (if unlikely) habitat. There is an intimation, within Renewal, that if past success has revolved around the notion of "getting what we want," then current and future happiness may come to have more to do with "wanting what we have."

Renewal can reach us—and reaches out for us—along many unlikely pathways, and in many guises. It is, indeed, strange to find that Renewal can, at times, present itself to us as a companionable presence. It is as if an absolute shift in life-phase has occurred, and *this shift colors everything.* Ambient mood starts to recalibrate to this development, and comes to assume that Renewal is now a "given"—has now become our starting point—our point of reference. We realize that we have lived our way out of damnation and into mercy.

Sometimes surprising surges of energy, felt as almost alien or long-vestigial, can appear without prior notice, awakening us to what it actually feels like to be *energized!* Some core experience of our being is just suddenly *there*, and the effect can be utterly startling, especially when encountered as an exclusively inner-arising experience. Something is definitely brewing. Part of what may startle is not only the unheralded suddenness of such a surge, but the simultaneous recognition of a quality within the surge itself that is quaintly familiar. This experience was—is—who we were, once upon a time ... and now *it* has begun to find its way back to us—from its *own* exile! Such energized moments can, in the beginning of Renewal, be quite brief, with their significance not readily comprehensible amidst what may still be quite dismal external circumstances. However, this energy—this soft-boundaried rush, this formless flux—is, nonetheless, the intangible yet definite talisman of what has annealed within. Energy freed from past constraints and constrictions and conceptions, regardless of whether these challenges have been resolved or outlasted, is energy freed to fuel *us*—in all areas—including the formation of new identity, and the venturing of initiatives of any sort in the outer world which are such a part of who we are becoming.

It is this very energy that, in the fullness of Renewal, eventually enables us to follow the ancient admonition: "Take up thy bed and walk."

# PAEAN TO THE NEW YOU
*. . . (and some questions, too)*

You've made it through (and for those of you who have not yet — and don't see how you ever can — know that, in the fullness of time and in some yet-to-be-determined form, you will). *How could you?* The forces marshaled against you were so great and unrelenting. You counted yourself out — felt you were irretrievably "down for the count" — many, many times during the worst(s) of it (for there are many worst moments in any such siege), for timeless hours, countless days, unbroken weeks and dreary, unending months at a time. Within the contraction of fetal terror you were convinced that, despite your noble dreams, ardent aspirations and the conviction that you were supposed to have been divinely protected, your life was to be cast on the slag heap of the tragic: your collapse, another anonymous, meaningless defeat ciphered in the annals of humankind.

Yet the Universe, undaunted, has breathed new life into you, has unbent you, has raised you up from the damned, has given you new eyes to see. Through the dismemberment, you have developed fresh ways of perceiving and *knowing*. Once slain, you have learned to inhabit rarefied territory and to befriend, after a fashion, the nether regions. Utterly, utterly ready to die — to expel life — to have life at any level taken from you — on many occasions, *you yet lived*. And now, you abide in the knowledge that, *having lived Identity Death, no fright can cripple or annihilate you ever again*. You have been through the worst that (even worse than) you could possibly have imagined and — *not* because you've become numb, inert or insensate (for you know you haven't), but because you have been tested and tempered in such severe ways, have been baptized, bonked, burst open — you are led into a way of experiencing existence that is beyond all fear and terror, beyond all suffering and sorrow, beyond any narrow, intense form of loving, beyond any way of life you ever would have stood a chance of comprehending, let alone deemed desirable.

Yet here you are, now, still drawing breath, technically in a situation of triumph — a triumph of endurance, in a way — but not one to be vaunted over anything or anybody. The real triumph is of the spirit that animates you, that has pulled you off the slag-heap of the tragic and is refashioning and reinventing you.

And what form, now, is your reinvention taking? Have you regained all that was lost? Do reconciliations and reunions abound? Is prosperity arisen for you once again? Do you electively forgo any of the above through the minting of some inner mastery? Do you participate fully in any (or all) of the above, also through the minting of some inner mastery? Is restoration an all-or-nothing game for you — a black and white game? ... Or do you surf the grays in delight, and revel at the utter imprecision, messiness and ambiguity of it all? What does it all mean to you?

And how do you feel, having come through such an initiation? Do you have any sense of how rare it is — not, mind you, to be hit with the raw material of demise (for that is as common as crabgrass) — *but to have made it through consciously* — in a conscious way? ... And even, perhaps, having dared at times to confront one's Creator out of the very agony and rage of one's plight, of one's perdition — to have been in such meager, impoverished circumstances as to have had nothing further to lose by "sticking it in God's face," *and doing it*: perhaps, as yet, even helping, through the brazenness of so doing, to bring God Her/Himself to some form of greater consciousness—and conscience? (Did not Job's own vociferous complaints result in an audience?)

And what do you make of your life now? Yes, that teasing expression "make of your life," which can mean both "How do you *make sense of* your life?" and "What are you going to *do* with your life?" (You owe only yourself an answer to this one.)

Do you need to make, with the fullest commitment of your being, your life a living demonstration of some principle or ideal that you have come to hold dear?

And how does what you have been through shape your expectations about your relationship with whatever comes to you? Can you ever again, knowingly, take seriously the supposed immutability of *anything*? And if you know you can't, where does that leave you? Can love still breathe new life into your heart? (Does love flow from the heart? ... Or is the heart awakened by love?) Are you, even yet, really able to love and attach with zest, in the face of acknowledged impermanence, able to show up for something and somebody wholeheartedly—soulheartedly—knowing all the while that, within any instant, it could be there for the duration—or gone in a flicker?

Does the awareness of the transitory nature of all things have you cowering in reluctance at the prospect of forming the attachments of living and loving with that which may come into your life and adorn it for awhile? ... Or do you find an ultimate adventure in NOT holding back—in participating at robust levels of mind, body, spirit and heart with all that is before you, savoring of the richness of experience for its own sake, despite its utter impermanence? *Indeed, can you love another without making the apparent impermanence of holding love with another a self-fulfilling prophesy* (so that if you happen to get lucky and find your soul mate you don't have to act impetuously, screw things up, and foreclose on a situation that could, within the span of a lifetime, come to glow, and "go the distance")?

If your elective path runs more along ascetic lines, is your asceticism an outgrowth—an extension—of a fully lived and explored outer life?... Or is your abstentious path—your renunciation—rather, a preemptive avoidance of venturing forth, a wholesale retreat from the world?

And through all of this, what becomes of your relationship with YOU—likely the most enduring one you will ever know directly within this lifetime? Has anything new been coined there? Do you hate what it is you have been obliged to face even as you come to love YOU for the way you face things? Is all in the outer world a mirrored stage on which you play out the refinement of your relationship with YOU—perhaps the ultimate intimacy—the ultimate romance?

Do you yet cling to whatever comes to you?... And, alternately, are you sometimes aware (having made it through the mill) of having discovered any new-found, internal source of knowing who you are and what you are about, which *frees* you to love yourself as YOU—to experience yourself as YOU—to know your life as truly *yours*?... And are others who have come into your life during your restoration just the holders of mirrors up to you from which facets of yourself—your own being—are flashed back and revealed to you (as necessary as this may be)?... Or has the freedom of discovering your own separate center of gravity—your own inner anchorage—opened you to true revelation: that of experiencing another person as an irreducible *other*, a circumstance that has you finding yourself, at times, reveling in the utter, unassailable, inalienable, *individual* nature of another—another's own sanctified being—freed from any need to attempt to fold, spindle, mutilate, manipulate, control, distend, bend-to-the-will, or otherwise "change" them?—*without* having to engage in any campaign to transmogrify yourself (to meld with another) or to change another (to meld with you)? Have you discovered the richness of mutual dependence and interdependence, in contradistinction to "co-dependence?"

And whatever it is that comes to you (and regardless of whether you "cop to a case of the clingies" or not), can you, above and beyond any drama of the immediate moment, wear it all like some loose garment and simply appreciate it—appreciate having it ... appreciate having ... appreciate? Can you appreciate your life?

How *are* you doing? (If you're doing well, you're doing "you.")

And how (if at all) have your attitude and perspective changed on what you observe in the lives of so many others—their struggles and strivings, their (at times) extraordinary outer-world successes, their private passions and besetting evils, their personal hells, their kindnesses, their sensitivities, their heroism? Has envy, or any of the sterner passions, given way, at all, to compassion? Is the distinction (and boundary) between "compassion" and "passion" clear to you? Do you observe, and acknowledge, a larger picture affecting those about you—*even those who would cast you as their enemy*?

How do you carry yourself, in the world, now? And *whom*, now, do you carry *within* yourself? Who else within you is welcomed to be there—is capable of peering out at the world through those eyes of yours, or listening in through your ears, or sensing through your skin? (Or are you, rather, *their* guest—a borrower of *their* senses?) If you are the reality the other person faces, what reality are others encountering when they encounter YOU? What flows from you? What is your issuance?

And how do you now define yourself in terms of success or failure? Are you both at once? ... or neither never? *What has initiation brought to you—brought you to?* Do you feel any inclination or responsibility to share who and what you are become with the larger humanity which is us all? ... Or is your own becoming a private, sacred matter only, something to be developed, lived out and cherished in the relative anonymity of personal solitude?

What is your understanding about what befell you? Has this understanding evolved? For instance, were you obliged to encounter catastrophe despite possessing an apparently unblemished life (having the legitimate fruits of "right living" wiped out)? ... Or were you the target of your own undoing? Do you think that it makes a difference whether calamity is visited upon one, or whether one is the architect of one's own demolition? Does God still "keep score" on you? ... And do you "keep score" on God? Have you lived your way out of—come out from under—the sense of being divinely cursed?

And how would you advise others, if asked about calamity? Would you say that it is desirable, in the long run, to have been slain by it? ... Or would you say that the outcome from such a grinding—such a protracted soul-jolt—may never be worth the pain that was exacted, along the way, by the process of identity dismemberment itself? Would you ever advise another to look for the experience? ... Or would you counsel, rather, that it is not we who seek the experience, but we who are overtaken by it (and therefore there is no reason to look for it)?

And how do you deal, now, with those who have neither the capacity nor the inclination for insight, those who have no vested interest in comprehending the scope and significance of what you have been through — and come through — those who are a vexation, whose habitual response to you is to judge you along the lines of how, in conventional terms, you have failed, or screwed up, or otherwise fallen short, or "had it coming to you" (often drawing on very ancient history, indeed)? Or those of historically sadistic bearing who lull you into "tender traps," summoning forth your, at times, still naively hopeful, trusting heart, only to (once again) nail you blindside? Are you still "hookable" into anger or rage-based exchanges with those who would provoke you and scorn you? ... Or are you quite resistant to being depth-charged, and (relatively) immune to reacting from a place of rage on those occasions when you are actually subjected to intense provocation? ... And when you discover, periodically, that you are still capable of feeling the throbbing, impetuous pounding pulse of rage, can you accept that in yourself without hating yourself too much?

Is there any depression-based cowering left in you? ... Do you still live with the possibility that you could "pull a nutty?" ... And what if you did? Is this the end, something that undoes all that has now been created anew in you — the new you? ... Or is your latitude of self wide enough now to encompass ranges of energy and being that, within some proportion, are deserving and worthy of expression, regardless of how "off-scene" or "not your real self" (as assessed by others) they may appear? (For, after all, they are *all* a part of your inner family.) Do you assume — take up — the responsibility of providing opportunities (channels, outlets) through which these many different sides can emanate from you, and find useful, meaningful (and safe) ranges of realization in the outer world?

And are you able to observe YOU, through all this, to drop back and assume an "aesthetic perspective"—to "stand outside" (simultaneous to being immersed in) whatever is rocking your boat, whatever is pelting you or enthralling you (regardless of whether the source seems to be from within, or without, or both together)? Can you continue to learn from whoever or whatever is coming at you (from the outside) or expressing itself (themselves) through you—through your form (from the inside)—regardless of your consent? Can *you* assent to all this?

What a richness it would be if those of us who have come through the hellfires of calamity, the scourge of identity death, the healing desolation of life in the wilderness, the quickening pulse of renewal, and the sure knowledge of deliverance-realized could share our individual versions of this age-old passage with one another! What a treasure-bearing lode would be contained in such thoroughly human responses to all these previous questions (and so many others besides) from those who have been obliged to undergo the torments, and have made it through to tell the tale! Why, perhaps we might even tease the veil a bit, with levity, luring it away to reveal, beneath, so much that, to the untrained eye and untried soul, appears hidden and inaccessible (but is not!). Perhaps we could all exult at finding, within a community of kindred spirits, a resonance and a reassurance born of the affirming revelation that all our remarkable, highly personal and precious experiences are but endlessly individual variations on this underlying, universal, and ultimately unifying theme.

May you wear the blessings of your new life and being generously, and may many others be the beneficiaries of that Grace which has reached you.

On this hopeful note this little book — this little verbal melody — trails off...

Will anyone else pick up the tune?

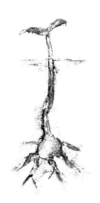

## About the Author

Stephen Rich Merriman lived in New England for nearly 61 years. He is, at the time of the publishing of this book, experimenting with making a life for himself in San Francisco. He is happily married, and living fully as person, husband, father and grandfather. He maintains staunch ties with his beloved New England.

# NOTES

# Notes

# Notes

Printed in the United States
209469BV00001B/20/P